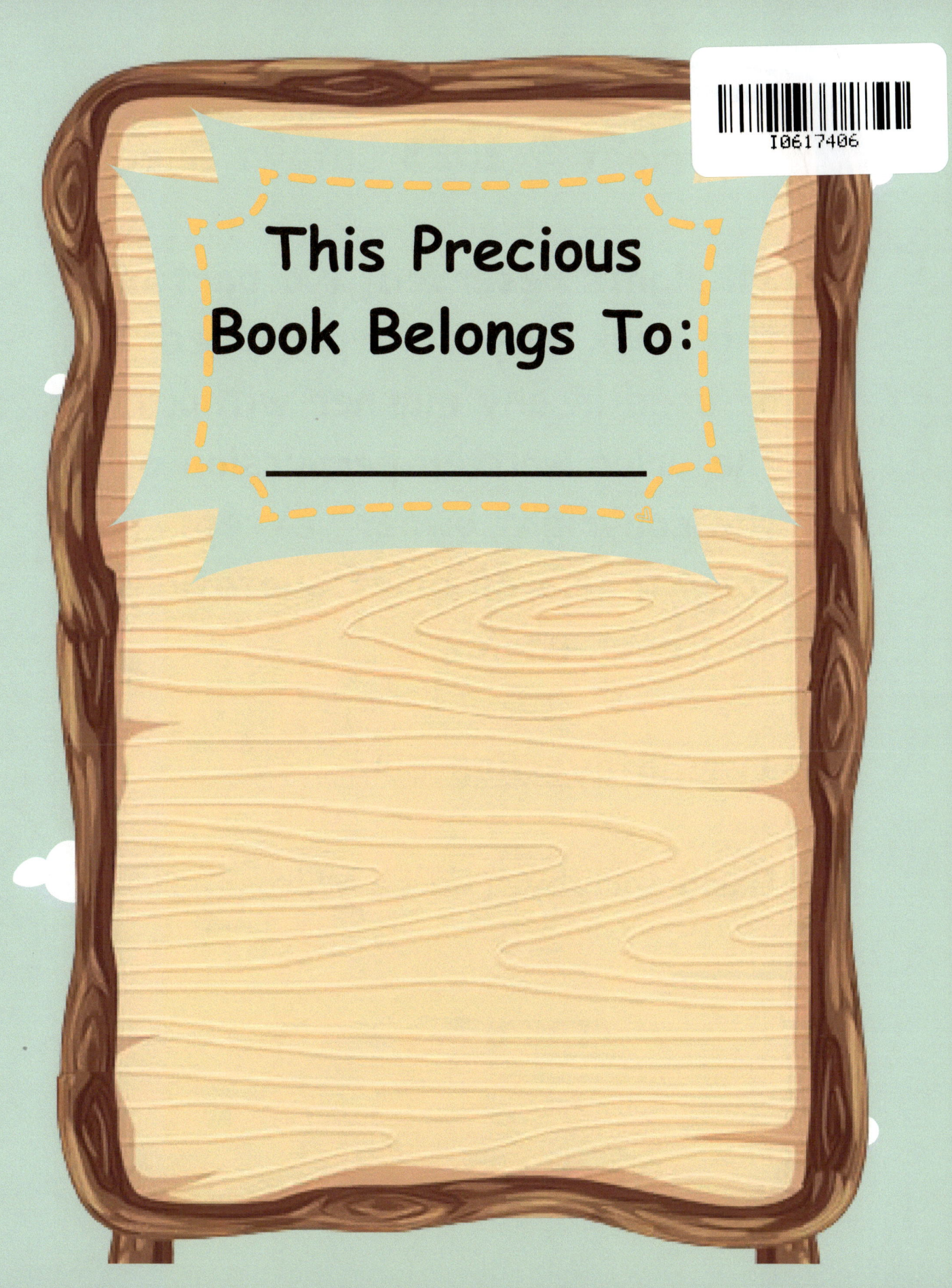

This Precious
Book Belongs To:

_____

Draw a picture of all the animals and people that Jesus created that you love below:

In a quiet town called Bethlehem, snuggled among rolling hills, there stood a stable, old and wise.

It was here, in this quiet place, that a story of hope was about to unfold.

Long ago, in a land far away, a young couple named Mary and Joseph embarked on a journey.

Mary, with a heart full of kindness, carried within her a treasure beyond measure - a baby named Jesus, sent by God to bring light to the world.

As the night draped its veil over Bethlehem, a radiant star emerged in the sky, its brilliance reaching out to lands near and far. Wise men, guided by this heavenly beam, followed its light to the stable, bearing gifts of gold, frankincense, and myrrh.

These are symbols that tell of the extraordinary destiny that awaited the child.

Nearby, in the fields, shepherds watched over their flocks under the vast expanse of the night sky.

Suddenly, an angel appeared, illuminating the darkness with a heavenly glow. The angel shared joyous tidings of Jesus' birth, proclaiming peace and hope for all people.

The shepherds were filled with awe and wonder. They left their sheep and hastened to the stable, drawn by the promise of hope.

There, they knelt before Jesus, offering their simple gifts of love and gratitude.

From that moment on, the world began to change.

Jesus grew in wisdom and kindness, teaching everyone He met about God, His love, compassion, and forgiveness.

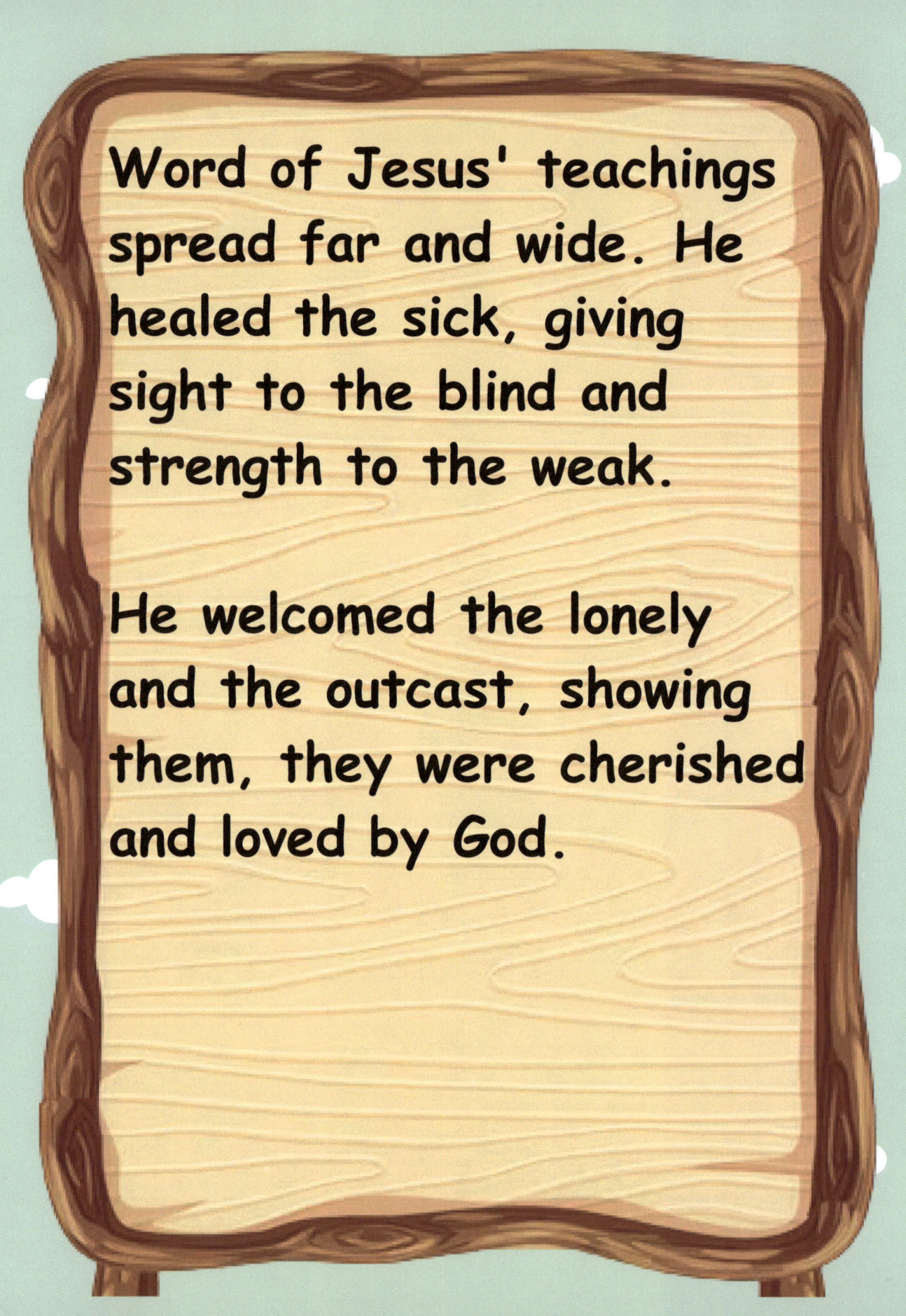

Word of Jesus' teachings spread far and wide. He healed the sick, giving sight to the blind and strength to the weak.

He welcomed the lonely and the outcast, showing them, they were cherished and loved by God.

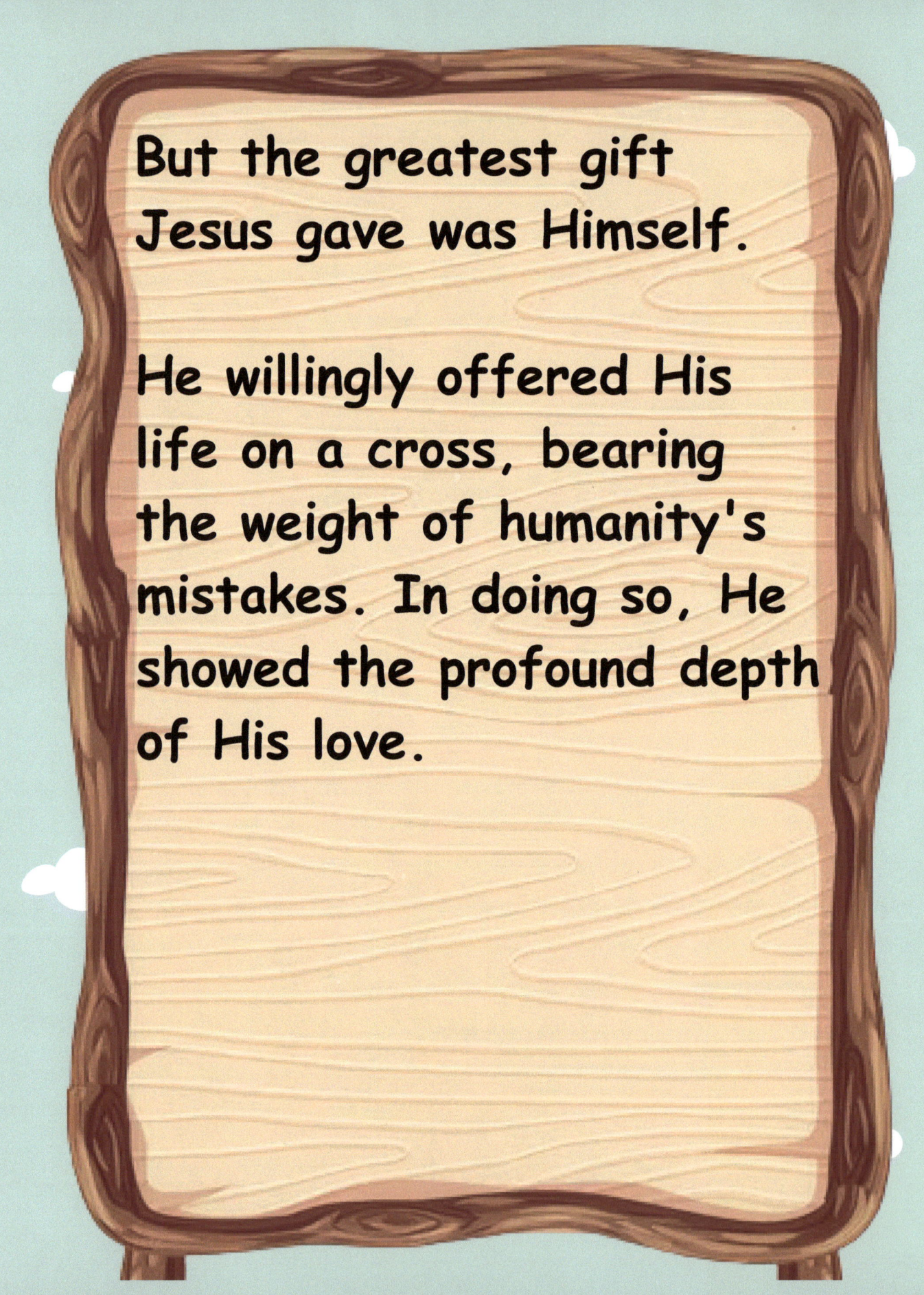

But the greatest gift Jesus gave was Himself.

He willingly offered His life on a cross, bearing the weight of humanity's mistakes. In doing so, He showed the profound depth of His love.

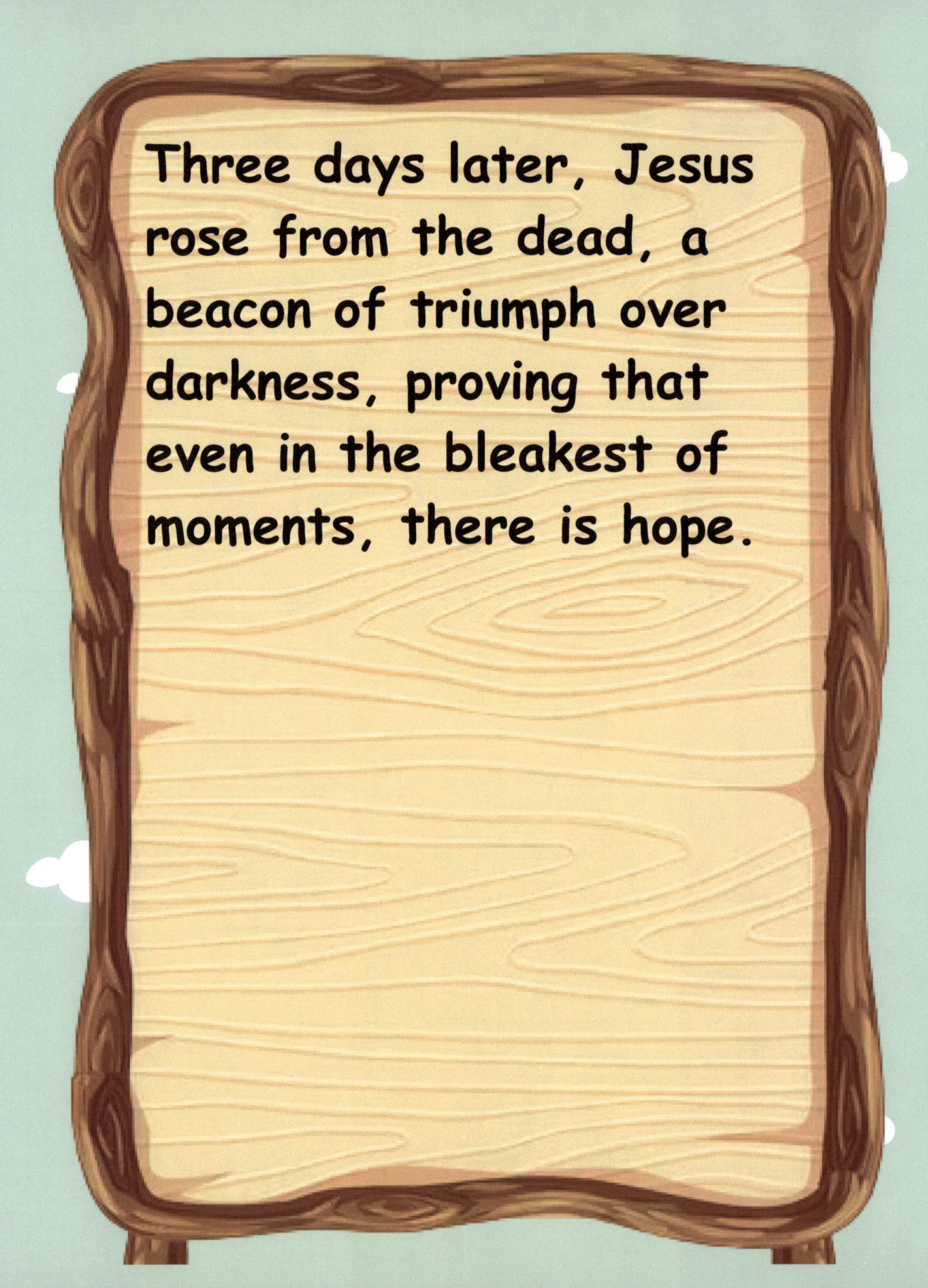

Three days later, Jesus rose from the dead, a beacon of triumph over darkness, proving that even in the bleakest of moments, there is hope.

He ascended to Heaven, leaving behind a legacy of love and salvation for all who believe.

And so, from that humble stable in Bethlehem to the majesty of Heaven's throne, the story of Jesus continues to inspire hope and light in the hearts of children and adults alike. Reminding us all that no matter the trials we face, there is always a glimmer of hope that awaits us when we believe in Jesus.

Remember, dear children, that just as Jesus' story began in a manger, your own journey is filled with opportunities for hope and transformation.

No matter what you've been through, there is always a path to a brighter tomorrow with Jesus. Embrace each day with kindness, love, and the knowledge that you are cherished beyond measure by God.

For in the story of Christmas, we find the greatest gift of all - the gift of unwavering love and light, shining bright in even the darkest nights.

Write below how you will share the greatest gift of Jesus today?

I'd love to hear your thoughts. Scan below to leave a review or to share with someone who could use this beacon of light.